PET OWNER'S GUIDE TO THE
CHINCHILLA

Natalie Kirkiewicz
& Gary Broomhead

RINGPRESS

ABOUT THE AUTHORS

Gary Broomhead and Natalie Kirkiewicz have kept chinchillas for many years, and have become fascinated by these captivating small animals. They have made a special study of the chinchilla's origins, which has led to a wider understanding of breed characteristics and the specific needs of the chinchilla when kept in a domestic environment.

ACKNOWLEDGEMENTS

We would like to give our thanks to Mr R. Bale and Mr and Mrs R. Ratcliffe for providing us with additional relevant information and for their support in writing this book.

Photography: Amanda Bulbeck

Published by Ringpress Books Limited,
PO Box 8, Lydney, Gloucestershire,
GL15 6YD, United Kingdom.

First published 1998
©1998 Ringpress Books Limited. All rights reserved

ISBN 1 86054 063 5

Printed in HONG KONG

CONTENTS

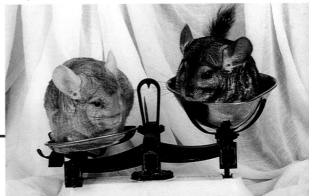

ABOVE:
Chinchillas were
originally bred for
their pelts, but
they are becoming
increasingly
popular as pets.

LEFT: Even
though they are
small, chinchillas
still require care
and attention.

Introducing the Chinchilla

This book is a complete, step-by-step, easy and comprehensive guide to buying, looking after, feeding and breeding chinchillas.

It is very important to remember before buying any pet, whether it be a dog, cat, rabbit or chinchilla, that it will need a great deal of love, care and attention from you. However, whereas the larger pets, such as dogs and cats, can roam around the house freely, it is not advisable to allow small mammals such as the chinchilla to roam in this way. They will tend to hide in dark places, for example behind fridges, radiators and cupboards, or even in washing machines! This could result in the death of your chinchilla through suffocation, starvation or even stress.

THE SMALLER PET

Smaller pets can be somewhat demanding, as they require feeding at specific times and their bedding changed regularly, but they are also very rewarding. Before buying any small pet such as a chinchilla, whether it be for yourself or for a member of your family, you must be prepared to dedicate a lot of time and energy, and you will need to provide a good-sized cage if the animal is to have a long and happy life.

Chinchillas are relatively new to the pet world. Most people are more familiar with rabbits, guinea pigs, hamsters and gerbils, and perhaps very few people have seen a chinchilla or know what they look like. This is because they have been bred for their splendid pelts (coats) for decades, which we will discuss in depth later, but it is safe to say that they make excellent pets and are not only cute to look at but fun to watch. They enjoy being showered with affection. We hope this book will help to provide answers to the many questions you may have regarding chinchillas and how to care for them in the best way possible.

WHAT IS A CHINCHILLA?

Chinchillas are actually rodents. Rodents are gnawing animals, such as mice and rats, but chinchillas look very much like rabbits – there is in fact a breed of rabbit called the Chinchilla Rabbit. Chinchillas differ from other rodents in that they have a big furry tail, like a squirrel's, which is normally about 3-11 inches long.

While most chinchillas have an abundance of compact, blue-grey fur which is more than an inch long, some have brownish-grey fur with light black markings. Compared with other mammals, chinchillas have much more fur per square inch on their bodies. Underneath, their fur is often yellowy-white. Their facial features include the standard large black eyes, large ears (which, incidentally, do not have very much fur on them) and very long whiskers.

Newly born chinchillas have their own teeth, consisting of two incisors or front teeth on the top and bottom jaws. They do not have any canine teeth, but they do have a few back teeth. Adult chinchillas can be as long as 12 inches with a weight of anything between 17 and 35 ounces. The females are sometimes called 'does' and are larger than the males, which are commonly referred to as 'bucks'.

ORIGINS

Chinchillas originated in South America, where they were native to the snow-capped mountains of the Andes. Here, they made their homes in gaps and crevices between very large rocks, and covered a wide area down the western side of South America in countries such as Chile, Bolivia and Peru at altitudes ranging from approximately 3,000 feet to as high as 15,000 feet. In such high altitudes, these little wild creatures would have been accustomed to fluctuations in climate and temperature, and, of course, their thick coats would have protected them against the cold. The chinchillas found in pet shops have been bred in captivity and hence have now become accustomed to different living environments, diets and climatic changes. Captive-bred chinchillas would not be able to live in the wild because they have come to rely on their owners for food, warmth and other comforts, and for this reason their daily regime must be maintained in order for them to survive. We will discuss this thoroughly in the following chapters.

For all animal lovers, it is very hard to comprehend that in the 1500s, when chinchillas were first discovered by Spanish pioneers, they were actually used as food by the native Chinca and Inca people of South America. The pioneers decided to name these little animals 'chinchillas', after the

Chincas, and later brought them back to the European continent – which nearly resulted in the extinction of the chinchilla.

THE PELT TRADE
In the years that followed, their increase in popularity and the subsequent use of their fur for the clothing trade, particularly for royalty within Europe, meant that the existence of the chinchilla was in jeopardy. Had it not been for the intervention of a man called

A member of the rodent family, the chinchilla is characterised by its profuse coat, its large eyes and ears, and its long whiskers.

Mathias F. Chapman, the American chinchilla would undoubtedly be a thing of the past.

In the early 1900s, Chapman, a mining engineer, was responsible for taking eleven captured chinchillas to the North American state of California, where he successfully began breeding them after conducting several tests on various living quarters and types of diet. Chapman did not breed the chinchillas as pets because he saw a potential niche in the market for their fabulous pelts.

Within forty years, the chinchilla fur trade was widespread across the USA. Even though some ranch owners thought about the possibility of having chinchillas as pets, Chapman never even considered breeding them for the pet trade. He had become successful in his breeding and selling of chinchillas for the fashion industry.

Although there are no chinchilla ranches or farms on a similar scale in Britain, there are quite a number of people who have come to love these furry animals and

Originating from the Andes, chinchillas needed their thick fur coats as protection against the harsh weather.

breed them as pets. Interestingly, there have been some sightings of chinchillas living freely in the wild in parts of Scotland and the north of England.

FROM PELTS TO PETS
Throughout the years, chinchillas have been well known for their fabulous, soft, thick, blue-grey fur, so it is perhaps not surprising that for many decades they have been bred in numerous parts of the USA purely for their pelts.

Most pet owners would probably find this fact very alarming, and might challenge the reason behind such an industry. At present, there are over 3,000 chinchilla ranches in the USA. Over the years, the public has been educated about the chinchilla, and has come to regard the animal as a potential pet, and not just as a fur-bearing animal. Unfortunately, however, most of the chinchillas bred on American ranches have ended their days as part of a coat or some type of clothing accessory such as a winter muff or handbag.

It is important to be aware that chinchillas sold in pet shops were bred for the sole purpose of being pets and never for their pelts.

ABOVE: Grey: The standard colour for chinchillas.

LEFT: Black Velvet: Note the dark markings around the head, neck and shoulder.

2 Breeds and Characteristics

There are two types of chinchilla – Chinchilla Brevicaudata and Chinchilla Lanigera. There are very few differences – both have large hind legs, which they often use to stand upright, and smaller front legs. The undersides of their paws are padded and they have only four toes and an underdeveloped thumb.

Brevicaudata: Of the two types, the Brevicaudata has a thicker neck and shoulders, making it appear bigger than the Lanigera. It is the longer of the two, but despite this, has the shorter tail.

Lanigera: The Lanigeraís distinguishing features are its angular face and pointed nose. Despite this slim, long look, the Lanigera is smaller than the Brevicaudata. Experts agree that domesticated chinchillas are of the type Chinchilla Lanigera.

CHINCHILLA BREEDS

The various chinchilla breeds are basically recognised by their different colours or mutations. Their colour varieties are the result of the work of very experienced American breeders, who have experimented with inbreeding since the 1950s. The colours of the chinchillas are the product of genetic mutations normally caused by inbreeding. It is far too complex a subject to explain in great detail, but we will try to give an idea of what colour combinations are mated to produce different-coloured offspring. Inbreeding may also affect the density of the fur and guard hairs, altering the elasticity and softness of the fur, the patterns of the fur and the extent of the markings on the head, neck and shoulders of the chinchilla. These are not always positive, and it is a known fact that many inbred chinchillas have suffered from fur biting and often become infertile. Inbreeding became particularly popular purely for the production of fur for the fur trade, which is why it really does

Silver White: The result of mating white with blue-grey.

not bear much relevance to the average breeder of domestic pet chinchillas.

It is important to bear in mind that this type of breeding is only for very experienced breeders who not only have the skill, tolerance and money to carry out these sort of experiments, but also have an awareness of the many risks involved. This type of breeding should never be experimented with by novice breeders.

Here are a few examples of the different-coloured chinchillas which were mated to produce different-coloured offspring, otherwise known as mutations.

WHITE: When the American breeder, Wilson, bred the first white chinchilla, it was from parents who were both the standard blue-grey colour and was something which had never happened before. It was then found that if a white male was mated with a standard blue-grey female, a high percentage of the offspring were white.

SILVER WHITE/PLATINUM: Mating white chinchillas with blue-grey chinchillas would often produce silver white and platinum offspring.

ROSE/APRICOT: Mating beige chinchillas with white chinchillas gave rise to cream-coloured offspring known as rose or apricot.

BLUE BLACK VELVET:

Mating black velvet chinchillas with clear blue-grey chinchillas produced offspring known as blue black velvet, which was considered to be the most beautiful colour by the fur traders.

PASTEL/BROWN/SAPPHIRE VELVETS:

Mating black males with females of varying colours produced offspring such as pastel velvets, brown velvets and sapphire velvets.

COLOURS

The standard colour of a chinchilla is blue-grey, but this is normally broken down into three markings which form the so-called 'agouti' pattern. They are the undercoat or underfur; the middle colour; and the markings around the head, neck and shoulders. Chinchilla fur also has 'guard hairs', which are hairs which stick out from the undercoat by a few millimetres, and give the pelt its elasticity.

Normally the abdomen is white or light grey. However, as described above, Wilson developed the white in 1955, and

Beige: Mating two beiges can produce dark-beige or rose-coloured offspring.

Brown velvet: The result of mating a black male with a female of a varying colour.

in 1956 a fellow American called Gunning developed the black velvet chinchilla. Other colour varieties include charcoal, beige, rose or apricot, chocolate brown, silver, platinum, pink/white, mosaic, brown velvet, pastel velvet, sapphire velvet, blue black velvet and even albino.

Chinchillas usually have the standard black eyes, but some have been known to have ruby eyes.

BLACK VELVET
Black velvet chinchillas have fur which has a black undercoat, a thin grey/white middle colour and dark black markings around the head, neck and shoulders.

SILVER
Silver chinchillas have a silver-grey undercoat, a white middle colour and silver-grey markings around the head, neck and shoulders.

WHITE
White chinchillas have fur which is either all white, or white with black guard hairs

PLATINUM
Platinum chinchillas have a light blue undercoat, a bluish-white middle colour and bluish markings around the head, neck and shoulders.

SAPPHIRE
Sapphire chinchillas have a light blue undercoat, a blue/white middle colour and light blue markings around the head, neck and shoulders.

ROSE OR APRICOT
The fur on these chinchillas is cream.

CHOCOLATE BROWN
Chocolate brown chinchillas have a very deep dark brown undercoat, a light brown middle colour, black-brown markings around the head, neck and shoulders and a brown abdomen/belly.

ALBINO
Albino chinchillas are pure white and have red eyes.

TEMPERAMENT
Although well known for their mild and friendly temperament, chinchillas will bite if scared or provoked in any way, and they have sharp teeth which can inflict quite a lot of harm. Chinchillas may become a little aggressive if

Mosaic: This variety has distinctive colour band markings.

they are not held in the correct way, which should be firmly. Chinchillas may actually feel scared and shed their own fur if

they are held incorrectly. This firm hold gives the animal a sense of security. Once they become accustomed to you they will enjoy being stroked and held just like any other pet, but do not be too disheartened if it takes some time for the chinchilla to get used to you.

HYGIENE
Chinchillas are extremely hygienic animals and they do not have a

Albino: Note the red eyes.

distinctive odour unless they become frightened, in which case the smell is one which can only be described as a very sharp burnt almond odour. Inside the chinchilla's anus there is a gland from which the odour is sprayed. If a female chinchilla becomes scared or feels threatened in some way, she has an added deterrent – she stands up on her hind legs and shoots urine at the offender. For those people who breed chinchillas, this can often happen when the female rejects her intended mate.

VOCAL SOUNDS
Chinchillas are often vocal, but this is normally only a chirping noise. On occasions, they have been heard to whine or yelp. These sounds, however, have no real significance. Perhaps they can be compared to the sounds that other animals, such as cats and dogs, make – no-one really knows what all their vocal noises mean either. When chinchillas are angry they make a loud clicking noise. Their warning signal sounds like "key key"

NOCTURNAL HABITS
Chinchillas are nocturnal, which means that they sleep in the day, . and are awake during the evening, when they tend to play and run around the cage with plenty of energy and enthusiasm. During the day, if they are awake, they will tend to just sit quietly, resting after a long night's play.

LIFESPAN
On average, it has been found that chinchillas who live freely in the wild can live for up to ten years. Although it has been known for some to live for as long as 20 years in a cage, they generally live for about 9-10 years as a household pet.

MIXING
Chinchillas should be kept away from other pets, such as dogs and cats, which could pose some

Watch out!: Chinchillas are great escape artists.

danger and cause undue stress to your chinchilla, which may ultimately lead to health problems. This is an important point to consider if you ever decide to ask a friend or neighbour to look after your chinchilla while you are on holiday. If they have any such pets in the house, you may find your chinchilla very distressed when you return.

ESCAPING
Chinchillas are very playful and inquisitive animals. They enjoy running and jumping and are very difficult to catch if they escape from their cage. This can be very dangerous as the chinchilla will hide in corners or behind furniture and under beds, and then begin to chew on things close by such as a chair leg, the carpet and even electrical leads from lamps, stereos and televisions. For this reason, it is important that you never leave the cage door open or the chinchilla unattended.

LEFT: Hold your chinchilla gently, but firmly.

BELOW: Some breeders lift chinchillas by their tails – but this is strictly for the experts.

3 *Buying Your Chinchilla*

Now that you have read the first chapters of this book and decided that you want one of these adorable animals as a pet, here are a few factors to remember when choosing and buying your chinchilla.

HANDLING

Always handle a chinchilla before buying it, as this will enable you not only to determine its nature but also to decide whether or not this is the right chinchilla for you. We will explain later how you can conduct a simple little health check on the chinchilla while it is being held, and this is of great importance. Often, it has been found that older chinchillas tend to be a bit hesitant when held as they have become quite stuck in their ways.

When approaching the chinchilla, ensure that your movements are slow and easy, and a soft tone in your voice will make the animal feel comfortable and less likely to be scared by any sudden gesture or loud noise. Chinchillas are fairly timid animals and may need some encouragement to come to the side of the cage.

Before attempting to lift the chinchilla out of the cage, it is wise to let it become accustomed to you and familiar with the scent of your hands. Be cautious as you do this and do not be tempted to pull your hand back suddenly for fear of being bitten. You must never be so bold as to just reach into the cage and attempt to remove the chinchilla, as it will not be expecting this and will most certainly try to bite to defend itself. Having said that, chinchillas tend to nibble rather than bite, unless of course they feel they are in a dangerous position.

When both you and the chinchilla feel comfortable with each other, you may lift it gently

Chinchillas become increasingly tame with handling.

if you do not lift the chinchilla in this way, but that you support the body quite firmly, which will make the chinchilla feel safe and increase its trust in you.

Just by holding the animal, you will not only be able to determine its temperament but also its state of health, which are two very important factors when choosing your pet. Once you have the chinchilla safely in your hands, you can conduct a quick and simple health check.

WEIGHT

When holding the animal, it should feel firm and have a weight of approximately 1-2.5 lbs if fully grown, which is normally around eight months of age.

AGE

Most chinchillas are fully weaned at 10-11 weeks, but the actual weaning process begins at 6-8 weeks. Studies have shown that, if the animal is separated from its mother when it is too young and not completely weaned, it can become sick and even die. This is because some owners will tend to give their new pet adult food rations, which leads to the young chinchilla overfeeding, which can

out of the cage, making sure it sees you and is not frightened by a sudden movement from behind. Although some breeders actually lift chinchillas by their ears or by their tail, they also support the animal underneath the body so that the tip of the tail does not break off. We would suggest, however, that it is probably better

The chinchilla you buy should be at least 12 weeks of age.

result in death. Most fatalities occur some time between weaning and around three months of age. Chinchillas should be given half adult food rations until they are 5-6 months of age.

Although most people would probably want a young chinchilla, it is important to remember that they may not actually be ready to leave their mothers until they are at least 12 weeks old, and could suffer fatal consequences. This must be considered when choosing your new pet.

EYES
Next, check the eyes. The indicators of good health are if the eyes are sparkling and alert, not tired-looking, and they should have no visible signs of sores or scabs. If the eyes are watery, it is quite possible that the chinchilla has a problem with its teeth, which we will discuss later.

TEETH
Examining the teeth is a little more difficult, as most animals are not willing to open their mouths for inspection. A good way to overcome this problem is to give the chinchilla a treat, which will enable you to get a good look at its teeth as it chews on the food. You might think that pearl-white teeth are favourable and normal – however, this is not so. They should look as if they are almost

The eyes should be bright and sparkling.

stained a yellow or orange-yellow colour.

There could be a problem with the chinchilla's teeth if you notice that it dribbles from the sides of its mouth as it eats, or if the fur around the mouth is wet and tangled. This again makes it difficult for the chinchilla to eat and could lead to more serious health problems.

DROPPINGS

It might seem strange to want to view the chinchilla's droppings, but this is a very good indicator as to its state of health. Although there is no such thing as 'normal' droppings, they should be a brown-green colour. They should be of the same size, with a shape which is long and rounded, and slightly damp. A problem with the digestive system is indicated if there are empty holes inside the droppings which have been split open, because this is where undigested food collects, or if the droppings appear longer and more angular with a sort of sticky substance covering them. It is quite common for a chinchilla to eat part of its droppings, as this helps to keep a certain level of bacteria in the digestive system.

DUST BATH

Finally, you will need to take a good look at their dust bath. Check that it is either being used

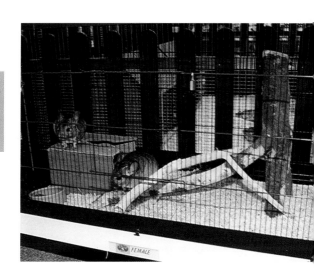

or has been used, as it is good for their fur and it is not possible to encourage chinchillas who are out of the habit of dust bathing, or who have never had a dust bath, to use one.

Chinchillas prefer to bathe in a type of fine crushed powder/sand (which we will discuss later) as opposed to having a wet bath. Since they are nocturnal, chinchillas will tend to bathe very early in the morning because during the night they will have been jumping, running around and playing in their cage, causing their fur to become untidy. The purpose of the dust bath is primarily to clean the chinchillas' fur as they roll around in the

powder. It removes excess oil and grease and generally helps to maintain a healthy-looking coat. Perhaps we could compare this to people shampooing their hair for basically the same reasons.

MALE OR FEMALE?

There are no strong reasons for choosing either male or female, as there is no difference in terms of temperament and looks. However, if you want a pair, it is important not to have two chinchillas of the same sex, as they will not get on together when in a cage.

It is best to have a pair who have already spent some considerable time living together in the same quarters, for example

If you plan to keep two chinchillas, make sure they are of the opposite sex.

at the pet shop, but if this is not possible they must be introduced to each other slowly before they share a cage. This initially will mean separate cages placed side by side for a while. This will allow the chinchillas to observe each other and to become familiar with each other's scent. This is also an important factor when attempting to breed chinchillas, which we will discuss in Chapter Seven.

4 Setting Up Home

Home is where the heart is, the saying goes. We all like the comforts of our own home and why should it be any different for your pet? Remember that your chinchilla will spend most of its life in its home/cage, and so it is up to you to make it as comfortable and as pleasurable as possible. This, in turn, will help towards keeping your chinchilla happy and content. Here are some simple but very important steps to ensure that you provide the best home for your chinchilla.

THE CAGE

If you do not intend to breed chinchillas, then it is important for adult chinchillas to have separate cages because chinchillas of the same sex do not get on if housed together. The cage should not only be easy to clean but also of a good size, so that the animal

does not feel claustrophobic or unable to move around easily.

We suggest that the minimum size of your chinchilla's home should be 18-24 in (45-60 cm) deep, 24-36 in (60-90 cm) wide with a height of 18-24 in (45-60 cm). Wire mesh cages have proven to be very popular, and this is because they are easy to clean and are not likely to rust. The size of the wire mesh itself is an important factor if you want to be sure to keep the chinchilla

A solid-bottomed wire cage,

inside the cage. Remember that, if a female chinchilla has babies, they will escape if the holes in the mesh are too large. For this reason, they should be less than one square inch in size.

Although cages made from plastic-coated wire might initially appear practical, they are not, because the chinchilla will chew the plastic. Wooden cages are also less suitable because they become dirty and stained by the animal's urine, which is difficult to clean. They will therefore need to be replaced more often.

There are many types of cage which could be suitable for your pet, but we will only highlight two of them which, incidentally, are the most popular among chinchilla owners.

WIRE-BOTTOMED CAGE

Cages with wire bottoms have metal or plastic trays beneath them, which collect the droppings and excess food. The tray should be lined with newspaper and/or wood shavings, which are inexpensive but will need to be replaced every day or every other day to ensure that the cage is kept clean and the chinchilla comfortable. This removable tray is a speedy and efficient way of maintaining a clean environment for your pet and is less of a chore for whoever has to clean the chinchilla's cage.

SOLID-BOTTOMED CAGES

Cages which have solid bottoms seem to be the favourites because, although they too are easy to clean, the chinchilla appears to find them more comfortable. Unlike the wire-bottomed cages, these come with a box underneath them which can be pulled out whenever you need to change the wood shavings which should line the bottom of the cage.

USED CAGES

If your previous pet has died and you decide to use its cage to house a replacement, it is essential that you not only clean it thoroughly, but also disinfect it to avoid any build-up of bacteria which could be very harmful to your new pet. Once you have disinfected the whole area using a domestic disinfectant, it must be rinsed with lots of water. It must then be left to dry completely before placing another chinchilla in the cage.

Normally, with metal cages, a

Wood shavings are safe and comfortable.

domestic disinfectant will suffice, however 'burning' it out with a blowlamp (such as those used by plumbers, easily obtained from most DIY outlets) will ensure that all types of bacteria have been destroyed. It is important to remember that, if your cage has a plastic pull-out tray or base, you must remove it first before using the blowlamp, or it will melt!

WOOD SHAVINGS

Bags of wood shavings can be bought from any local pet shop and are relatively cheap. Although numerous tests have been carried out using other materials such as sawdust (an extremely fine material which could easily get into the eyes and nose of a chinchilla and cause great discomfort), sand, hay and straw, wood shavings have been found to be the most suitable and comfortable for chinchillas. It is very important, however, to choose ones which have not been treated, as chinchillas tend to chew the shavings and this could result in harm to the animal. Avoid using cedar wood shavings as the resin can be dangerous to your pet. If you are in any doubt about the type of wood shavings you are going to use, ask the owner of the pet shop for advice.

FOOD CONTAINER

In order to feed your chinchilla, you will need a bowl of some kind. The best types of bowls or food containers are metal and can just be slotted on to the side of the cage, which keeps the food fresh. They are also practical when you need to clean or refill the container as they avoid the unnecessary repetition of opening and closing the cage door.

Bowls on the floor of the cage are not recommended because they can easily be knocked over and are not very hygienic, and the chinchilla will tend to kick wood shavings into the food as it runs around the cage.

Food containers can be bought from any local pet shop in various sizes, so ask for advice if necessary.

A gravity-fed water bottle will provide a fresh supply of water. It must be changed daily.

WATER BOTTLE

Fresh, clean water is very important for the survival of such a small animal and by far the best way to provide this is by using a small glass- or metal-tubed bottle which, again, can be attached to the side of the cage in just the same way as the food container. These are the same types of water bottle often used for rabbits and guinea pigs and they have a ballpoint tube which prevents the water from leaking. These are often referred to as gravity bottles. Do not use a plastic-tubed bottle

as it will be chewed by the chinchilla. Do not use bowls or dishes for drinking water as it will not remain clean and fresh if left on the bottom of the cage. This is because the chinchilla will tend to kick bits of wood shavings, and maybe its droppings, into the bowl as it runs around the cage.

Always ensure that the water is changed daily to prevent the risk of bacteria building up in stale water. When cleaning the bottle, always use a mild form of washing-up liquid (or perhaps a sterilising solution as used for human babies), making sure you rinse it thoroughly – including the cap and tube. You may wish to buy a small bottle brush which some people have to clean their baby's bottle. This will allow you to clean it thoroughly, reaching right down to the bottom of the receptacle. The food dishes should be cleaned just as thoroughly, and always dispose of any uneaten food before refilling. Water bottles can also be bought from your local pet shop and they too come in different sizes.

CAGE LOCATION

Where you choose to put the cage is extremely important and can affect the health of your chinchilla. They do not like to be in temperatures which are above 80 degrees Fahrenheit (27 degrees Celsius). Not only do chinchillas become irritable and stressed at these temperatures, they may even die. On the other hand, do not put the cage where it will be subjected to cold or draughty conditions or where temperatures are likely to rise rapidly due to the heat of the sun. The room should be fully insulated, so, for this reason, garages are not ideal.

The type of room used to house the chinchilla is also important. If it tends to be a busy room which sees a lot of people or movement, or becomes very noisy during the day, then it is wise to cover the chinchilla's cage (as many owners do with their birds), and this will make it easier for the animal to sleep during the day and to adjust to its surroundings.

Because of fluctuations in the British climate, chinchillas should never be housed outside. However, the temperatures in late spring and early summer should be comfortable enough for your chinchilla to have a play in the garden, provided that you have a run of some kind, similar to those

Branches can be provided for climbing.

used for rabbits. Later we will discuss suitable outdoor runs.

TOYS

It is important that you provide your chinchilla with small wooden blocks, which your pet will chew to keep its teeth sharp and to prevent them overgrowing. The chinchilla will also use these blocks as toys, something to play with which will provide it with exercise.

Other items which might provide entertainment are exercise wheels and cardboard tubes. Cardboard tubes must be large, for example the inner tubes from rolls of carpet, or even large sections of plastic drainpipe, which can be purchased from your local DIY shop. Although these may seem simple to us, they are enjoyable play items for your pet. Some chinchilla owners put a small square piece of carpet in the cage, which the chinchilla will tend to sleep on, chew or even play with. If you can also find some thick branches to put in the cage it will jump, clamber up, play and chew these.

DUST BATH

Dust baths help to clean the chinchilla's coat by removing surplus oils, grease and any dampness, and they generally help to keep the fur looking healthy and in good condition. If two or more chinchillas share the same dust bath, this could increase the risk of diseases being spread, so each chinchilla should have one of his own.

The contents of the dust bath

Chinchillas are inquisitive animals and will enjoy toys to explore.

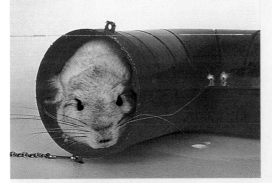

should be a fine crushed sand, which can be bought from a pet shop and is often referred to as chinchilla sand or silver sand. It is sold loosely or in bags and is inexpensive to buy. You must never use just ordinary sand as it tends to be gritty and sharp, which will irritate the chinchilla's skin.

The dust bath should be changed about twice a week and the droppings removed daily. You can allow your chinchilla

permanent access to a dust bath by leaving it in the cage, but remember that, the more baths the animal has, the more likely it is that the sand will become stained by urine. This rather defeats the purpose of the dust bath, so we would recommend that to maintain healthy, clean and unstained fur, you should change the sand more frequently if the bath remains in the cage.

It is important to remember that, if a chinchilla gets out of the

A dust-bath of fine, crushed sand must be provided. The sand can be sieved to keep it clean.

habit of having a dust bath, it is not possible to encourage it to have one again; baby/young chinchillas who never had a dust bath while they were being nursed will not take to using one after they have been weaned.

There are many types of containers which can be used as a dust bath, such as a cat litter tray or a metal box the size of a shoe box (or slightly larger), but if it is too big it will take up too much space in the cage and inhibit the movements of your pet. If you have any doubts whatsoever, the owner of the pet shop will be able to make the correct recommendations as well as suggesting other suitable toys for your chinchilla.

EXTRA COMFORT
An added comfort for your chinchilla is extra warmth, particularly in the cold winter months or if the room in which the cage is placed tends to get a bit cool. Near the radiator is an ideal place for the cage, but make sure that it is not directly against it for fear of causing heat

exhaustion and lethargy. It is wise to make sure that half the cage is warmed and the other half is cooler so that the chinchilla has a cool spot to go to if it gets too warm. Some owners and breeders like to use heat pads or lamps, but pads which are placed underneath the cage tend to dry out the urine, which causes odours and increases the possibility of bacteria developing. Heat lamps are perhaps preferable, but take extra care to ensure that the chinchilla cannot chew on the flex.

AN OUTDOOR RUN

Although outdoor runs are probably more commonly associated with rabbits, there is no reason why your chinchilla cannot enjoy the outdoor world – provided that it is not too cold or wet outside.

Your chinchilla will become very scared if approached by a cat or dog, which could cause it to suffer a great deal of stress, so we do not recommend that you give your pet an outside run if your garden receives these visitors. Be sure you never leave your chinchilla alone in case of any unexpected danger, or in case it becomes too hot and needs to rest in the cooler indoors. Any loud sounds or traffic noises may also frighten the animal.

The benefits of a run are many – the chinchilla has much more room to play, run, jump and explore than within the confines of its cage. A run provides it with an abundance of exercise and enjoyment. It is not recommended that you leave your chinchilla in the run for any great length of time, perhaps just 20-30 minutes is sufficient. A shady place on a hard surface, such as concrete, in the garden is ideal, as this will prevent the chinchilla from becoming exhausted and keep it away from any plants which may be poisonous and could harm it if eaten or chewed. Later, we will explain why green foods are not suitable for chinchillas, so you may wish to discourage your pet from exercising on the lawn.

You can purchase a rabbit-type run from most pet shops, or you can make one quite easily using wood and some strong wire, but make sure that it has some sort of lid so that your chinchilla cannot jump out and escape. Since chinchillas tend to burrow, you will need to ensure that the

An outside run will be enjoyed by your chinchilla.

bottom of the run is covered with wire, especially if you have placed the run on grass, otherwise you may find that it has dug a hole and escaped.

When your pet chinchilla is in its run is the ideal time to observe its many different characteristics and natural behaviour. The increase in space will encourage the animal to be more active and playful, and observing your pet as it plays in its run will provide you with entertainment and is one of the best ways in which to enjoy your pet.

So now your chinchilla is ready to move in to its newly furnished home!

5 Caring For Your Chinchilla

Grooming your chinchilla will not only help to maintain the beauty of its fur, but constant contact and attention will encourage the animal to get to know you and develop a sort of bond which is one of confidence and security. Keeping the chinchilla looking healthy and well-groomed is just as important as playing with it. Here are a few points to remember when you begin your grooming session.

SHEDDING
Chinchillas tend to shed their coats every three months or so, and you may well begin to notice small clusters of hair on the bottom of the cage. This shedding of the coat is perfectly normal and keeps the fur in the best possible condition – perhaps it could be compared to humans losing numerous hairs from their head daily to make room for new hair to grow. It is a good idea, although not absolutely essential, to periodically comb away the old fur to eliminate problems of cleanliness such as clumps of hair being left in the cage and, of course, to maintain the chinchilla's overall appearance.

The chinchilla sheds its coat every three months.

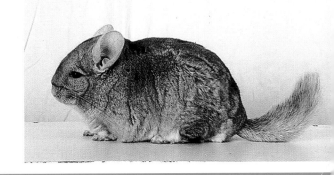

WHEN TO GROOM

It is best to comb the chinchilla just before it has a dust bath, because the separated fur will allow the dust to reach right down to the roots. Never comb the chinchilla immediately after a dust bath, because some of the dust will get caught on the comb and pull out perfectly good fur, resulting in an overall poor appearance as well as causing the animal a lot of pain.

HOW TO GROOM

The owner of the pet shop will be able to recommend two types of comb which you should use to groom your chinchilla, and both are inexpensive to buy. One is a wide-tooth comb and the other a fine-tooth comb.

It is easier if you use a hard surface such as a table, or perhaps a towel on your knee, to comb your chinchilla, but keep a tight hold on it so that it does not escape. Start the grooming process by using the wide-tooth comb and begin at the tail, working methodically and carefully until you reach its neck and shoulder area. Separate and comb small sections of fur and continue doing this down its back

The coat should be groomed with a wide-tooth comb followed by a fine-tooth comb.

and around the sides.

Next, use the fine-tooth comb in very much the same way, but try to part the hairs to a greater degree, which will loosen the fur. These small clumps of hair can be discarded. Do not be tempted to pull the fur as this will hurt the chinchilla; any loose hair will come out of its own accord. You may be concerned about the marks left on the fur from the comb but these will soon go when the chinchilla has a good shake and rolls around. When combing the chinchilla's belly, it is better if you sit down and have your pet lie on its back, on your lap. You will find that most chinchillas will enjoy being groomed, and, if they become a bit fidgety, try to alternate the areas which you are combing. The skin of a chinchilla is quite delicate so take care that you do not comb the fur too harshly or you may hurt the animal.

THE TAIL

You may find that the chinchilla's tail becomes stained by urine at the end and around the edges, or becomes too long. Taking extreme care you can use a sharp pair of scissors to remove any bits of fur which are stained or untidy, and, if you feel comfortable and confident, you can also trim the end of a tail which has become a little too long. Do this by holding the tail with your fingers and try to determine where the tail ends and the excess fur starts. Once you have established this, you can trim the end of the tail. This does not hurt the chinchilla in any way and is similar to people getting a haircut, but often the loud snipping sound from the scissors can frighten the animal and cause

The tail must be kept clean, and, in some cases, it may need trimming.

it to flinch or try to move away, so try to cut slowly and always have a firm hold of the chinchilla. Some chinchilla owners do not feel comfortable or happy about giving their pet a haircut, and, if this is the case with you, then it would be better to ask your vet to do this.

CLAWS

Occasionally, you may find that your pet chinchilla needs its claws trimming. To do this you will have to buy a pair of toenail clippers from the pet shop; do not use ordinary scissors. Make sure you have hold of the chinchilla very firmly – in fact, it might be a good idea to get someone to help you with this. When trimming the claws, take care not to cut the quick, which is the blood vein. Cut the claw about half a centimetre from the quick. This is often difficult to see if the claw is dark, so it is advisable to ask a vet or the owner of the pet shop to show you how to do this if it is your first time. Once again, if done correctly, this does not hurt the chinchilla in any way and I suppose is very similar to people cutting down their fingernails or toenails to keep them at an even

and comfortable length. However, if you are not comfortable or happy about trimming your pet's claws, ask your vet to do it.

FEEDING YOUR CHINCHILLA

PELLETS

Pellets can be obtained from any pet shop. They are often sold loosely by the pound, are inexpensive and provide essential nutrients such as vitamins and minerals. You will find them labelled as Chinchilla Pellets. Primarily, they are the staple diet of all chinchillas. Rabbit pellets, which may look very similar to chinchilla pellets, should never be given to your pet at any time. This is because they contain

Chinchilla pellets provide all the essential nutrients.

hormones which will tend to make the chinchilla fat, which could be fatal, and females may even be prevented from getting pregnant. Guinea pig pellets, however, are better as they contain similar ingredients to chinchilla pellets but they also have a lower fat content.

While at the pet shop, the chinchilla will have become accustomed to a particular diet and specific feeding times, so it is very important to maintain this regime, as any radical change might encourage the chinchilla to ignore its food and become prone to certain health problems. If you do change its diet in any way, it should be done gradually so that it really does not notice any difference. This can be done by adding small amounts of the new food to its regular food and then increasing the amount slightly until eventually it replaces the old supply of food.

Feeding chinchillas at the same time every day is particularly important and this is best carried out in the evening, when they are active and will be hungry. In the morning, they can be given just a small piece of dry bread or a slice of apple. If they are fed much later than their normal feeding time it has been known for some chinchillas to suffer from fits, or they may begin biting their own fur, resulting in health problems.

An adult chinchilla should be fed approximately 1-2 heaped tablespoonfuls of solid pellets per day.

WATER

Because the chinchilla's diet consists mainly of dry food, access to water is very, very important. A shortage will result in your chinchilla suffering from constipation, at the very least. Fresh spring water is the best to use, as chlorinated tap water can produce difficulties with fertility (unless of course your local authority does not add chlorine to its water). However, if you do use chlorinated water, it is better to boil it first and add a pinch of salt. You should give your chinchilla fresh water every day, discarding any left over from the day before.

HAY

Hay can be fed twice a day (morning and night), but do not give too much as the excess will be pulled out and build up on the

Hay can be fed twice a day.

bottom of the cage, which in turn becomes soiled by the animal's urine, increasing the risk of fungus developing. Hay, which must be of an acceptable standard, is a good source of roughage which contains a proportion of elements essential for the maintenance of a healthy digestive system. Not all hay types are suitable so, if fed the incorrect variety, your chinchilla could suffer harmful consequences. For this reason it is important to choose the right hay, and, if in any doubt, ask the owner of the pet shop for advice. The hay must always be absolutely dry – any moisture could result in diarrhoea for your chinchilla. Hay is sold in bags in all pet shops, and is fairly inexpensive to buy.

SPECIAL TREATS

Just as owners enjoy giving treats, chinchillas really enjoy receiving them. Once again, just as in the case of their normal food, it is very important to offer treats at regular times of the day, not to mix them with their normal food and never to give more than one type of treat at a time. Mixing the treats with the normal supply of food will only encourage the chinchilla to become fussy about what it eats. Try to wait a good few hours after they have eaten their main meal and, in order to avoid chinchillas refusing to eat

Sunflower seeds are considered a treat.

any pet shop, such as chocolate drops for chinchillas, rabbits and other small mammals, some others available are sunflower seeds, raisins (but only once or twice a week as they can be fattening), small pieces of apple and dry bread. Small quantities of dry, uncooked porridge are also a welcome treat. Always remove any uneaten treat at the end of the day so that the chinchilla never eats food which is not fresh.

their staple food of pellets, do not give more than one tablespoonful of treats a day. Apart from specific treats which can be obtained from

GREENS

There are mixed opinions about whether chinchillas should be fed greens of any kind because they

Chinchillas love raisins, but they are fattening.

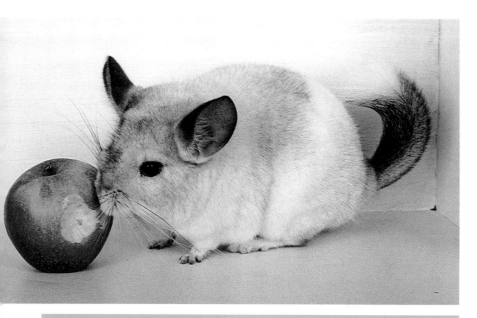

Apple can be offered on an occasional basis.

have quite sensitive stomachs. Many have suffered from diarrhoea and digestive problems, so it is better to avoid feeding your chinchilla greens at all. However, offering your pet the occasional piece of apple or potato will not do it any harm.

CIDER VINEGAR

This is sometimes added to the drinking water of chinchillas who are breeding and do not want to eat, or females who are very weak after they have given birth. The pure cider vinegar helps to create an appetite and so increases the animal's weight. Half a teaspoonful of vinegar should be added to 250 ml of water per animal, per day, until the chinchilla recovers.

6 Happy, Healthy Chinchillas

Chinchillas, on the whole, tend to be very healthy little animals and generally do not suffer many health problems if they have a clean cage, a well-balanced diet, a stress-free environment and lots of love and care. That is not to say that your chinchilla will never have any ailments or complaints, but, in order to avoid the problem escalating into something more serious, it is advisable that you conduct a little examination of the most important parts of the chinchilla's body every day. The quicker you deal with a problem, the quicker it will be treated and the chinchilla will not suffer undue stress or pain. In this chapter we have tried to highlight what to look for.

Remember that chinchillas are unable to tell you if they are in pain or sick, so you must watch out for signs of tiredness, refusal of food, loss of weight, poor condition of fur and some of the problems listed below. If in any doubt whatsoever as to your chinchilla's state of health, do not hesitate to take it to the vet.

Providing the correct care and diet should ensure that your chinchilla stays fit and healthy.

If you do ever need to take your chinchilla to the vet it is best to wrap it in a towel, not too tightly, which will not only assist in keeping the animal warm but also limit its movements and hence reduce the risk of it suffering from stress and, of course, of escaping. It is also advisable to use a towel in this way when examining a chinchilla for any ailments or health problems, because the constraints imposed by this wrapping-up will make the chinchilla feel secure and comfortable. If you follow these guidelines, and provide your chinchilla with a clean environment plus a regular and well-balanced diet and eliminate any stressful conditions, you will assist in ensuring it has a long, healthy and happy life. Always bear in mind that all pet animals rely on their owners to care for them and to ensure they remain healthy. They are unable to fend for themselves when small and kept in a cage and will constantly be your responsibility. Never ignore your pet or shy away from your duty and obligation as its owner, carer, provider, nurse and friend.

ROUTINE CARE

EYES
Healthy eyes should be clear and almost sparkling, but if they

If you handle your chinchilla on a regular basis, you will spot any signs of trouble at an early stage.

appear very dull and are watery, or if perhaps the eyelids are inflamed and sore, it could be a simple irritant such as a bit of dust, or even an infection – which must be treated with medicine from the vet. Sometimes, if the chinchilla's hay is damp, it can produce a type of fungus which will cause the eyes to be watery.

EARS
Most chinchillas do not suffer major problems with their ears, but if you notice any fluid coming out of the opening, or if the animal tends to bring its paw up to its ear time and time again or appears to almost have a loss of balance and direction, then you must take it to the vet right away. The vet will more than likely administer an antibiotic, which you will probably have to continue using once you bring the chinchilla back home. If this is the case, you must clean the cage thoroughly, and do not line it with wood shavings – use newspaper or a towel. Do not allow the chinchilla to have a dust bath until it is well again.

NOSE
If your chinchilla appears to have a runny nose but does not have any difficulty in breathing, this could simply be a normal cold. Just keeping the animal warm and ensuring that it drinks a lot of fresh water should be sufficient to clear the problem, but keep a careful eye on your pet's condition to make sure it does not develop into something worse. It is, once again, important to remember that, until the chinchilla is better, you should not allow it to have a dust bath.

MOUTH
Chinchilla teeth grow continuously at an incredible rate throughout their lives, which is why it is very important for them to have something to chew on all the time. This not only maintains sharpness but also prevents the teeth from overgrowing, which in turn reduces the risk of your pet suffering from dental problems. Overgrown teeth can prohibit the chinchilla from eating and hence it may become weak, lose weight and suffer from other illnesses.

The classic symptoms of a chinchilla having problems with its teeth, perhaps due to the fact that they are too long, are: a) the animal will tend to reach up to its

Gnawing fruit branches will help the teeth to wear down.

mouth with its paw many times; b) as it tries to eat some food it will dribble from the side of its mouth; and c) it may start losing weight. If the symptoms persist you must take it to the vet.

In order to minimise any dental problems, it is important to provide the animal with something to chew on at all times so that the front teeth remain sharp and straight. Chinchillas' incisors (front teeth) grow constantly throughout their lives, and, to prevent them from overgrowing, it is important to provide the animal with small wooden blocks (but it must be wood which has not been treated in any way as this could be poisonous) or branches from trees on which they can chew. If their teeth become too long it is difficult for them to eat and it may be necessary to file them down. If the chinchilla's teeth do become overgrown at any stage, we would suggest you take it to the vet who will show you the type of file to use and the correct way to use it. If the chinchilla has good, healthy teeth then they should be straight without any rough edges.

FUR

The intense compactness of chinchilla fur prohibits any type of parasite building a nest and so chinchillas very rarely suffer from any mites or other little pests. This is a bonus if you compare them to cats and dogs, which often suffer from ticks and fleas

Check the fur for matting or hair loss.

and require repeated medication to keep them under control.

If the animal develops a break-up of fur, this is due to a type of fungus which makes the hair look very messy and limp and could even result in the ends of the whiskers splitting and breaking, so it gives a poor overall appearance. More than likely, your vet will prescribe a type of fungicide which you will need to mix in the dust bath so that, as the chinchilla rolls around in the sand, the medicine will begin to work. It will normally take only a few days to clear and within a week new grey or white fur will appear.

Some chinchillas will bite their own fur, and although no-one really knows why, it is thought to occur if the animal suffers from stress brought on by poor living conditions, poor diet, irregular feeding times, damp or draughty conditions, too much noise or visits from cats and dogs. This is similar to when birds pluck out their own feathers. The 'tell-tale' signs to look out for are if the area of fur is tangled, wet or appears to be very short and almost bristly. Medicine is not always necessary; however you should examine closely its living conditions and diet. Avoid subjecting your chinchilla to any stressful conditions, such as placing its cage where it may be draughty or particularly noisy, or feeding it at irregular times.

If, on inspection, you discover there is a problem with any of the above, try to make any necessary changes very gradually so that it will give the chinchilla time to adapt and not cause any further undue stress. If you ever discover any small lesions or scratches on its skin they must be treated with antiseptic cream which will be recommended by your vet.

PNEUMONIA

One of the easiest ways of checking if your chinchilla has a fever is by simply touching its ears. It is quite possible that your chinchilla has a fever if its eyes are watery, but there is no visual evidence of any infection. It is very important to catch this in its early stages, as it could lead to pneumonia. Just as our normal body temperature is 98.6 degrees F, so is a chinchilla's. If the ears feel unusually warm and look a flushed red/pink colour then this is a good indicator. However, due to the way in which chinchillas often sleep – tucking their ears under their body – their ears may feel warm because of this, so wait a little while after your chinchilla has woken up before conducting your examination.

The onset of pneumonia may also be detected if the chinchilla finds it hard to breathe and tends to wheeze or has a runny nose. If this is the case, then your chinchilla will need to see a vet immediately because pneumonia tends to put a great deal of stress and strain on a chinchilla's body, and this could result in the death of the animal.

CONSTIPATION

This can be caused by numerous factors, such as the stress of bringing the chinchilla home from the pet shop, a long car journey, change in diet or not enough fresh water. The best way to check for this is by feeling the animal's abdomen (belly), which can be done by a vet. The belly will feel broader and the chinchilla may appear to be very tired or lethargic. A lack of droppings in the cage is also a good indication of constipation.

Constipation is also common in female chinchillas who are in the late stages of pregnancy. They will tend to suffer from it before and after giving birth, as some tend to eat the afterbirth, which causes digestive problems. Your vet will be able to recommend the correct treatment, which is often a medicine which you will need to mix in with its water, but on some

occasions it may be necessary to administer it straight into the chinchilla's mouth. For this, you can use a normal medicine dropper, which is very easy and effective to use. The following day it is important that you check the animal's droppings, which will indicate whether or not any more medicine is required. Constipation can also occur if the chinchilla is being given a mixed diet – this occurs when owners try to change the food but two types of pellets end up in the same food bowl.

When a chinchilla is constipated, you must ensure that it gets a lot of exercise, and this can be achieved by letting it out in a run of some kind, or in a small room where it cannot escape or hide in any dark corners. You may also wish to allow it to have more dust baths where it will roll around – this, too, is a form of exercise. Once again, try to avoid any sudden or major changes to the chinchilla's lifestyle, which will lessen the chances of health problems.

DIARRHOEA
This often occurs in young chinchillas who have a tendency to overeat, or in older ones who have eaten bad hay or food. Other

causes are stress, a change in the diet and too many green foods. The symptoms of diarrhoea are very loose or almost liquid droppings, and possibly a very wet or dirty patch around the animal's tail.

Once again, your vet will recommend the correct medicine, which may be in the form of a powder which should be added to the chinchilla's water, and it should only take a few days to clear up. Diarrhoea is one of the two most common ailments to affect chinchillas – constipation being the other.

ENTERITIS

If either of the two diarrhoea symptoms above are suffered for any length of time, it could be due to a problem with the chinchilla's intestine, where the intestinal tract becomes sore and inflamed. This is known as enteritis, and can be the result of an infection, food which has in some way irritated the chinchilla or by the prolonged use of antibiotics and is the result of many different types of bacteria. Symptoms to look out for in your chinchilla are: a) loss of interest in food and special treats, and an

inclination to ignore them; b) difficulty in walking; c) curling up into a little ball and just staying like that for some time.

If you detect your chinchilla displaying any of these symptoms, you must take it to a vet immediately.

HEAT PROSTRATION

Heat prostration is exhaustion or loss of strength due to excessive heat caused by an unsuitable cage location. It will give rise to your pet having difficulty in breathing, and it will simply lie down on one side and remain motionless. This is a very uncomfortable and stressful situation for your chinchilla to be subjected to. It is imperative that you take it somewhere cooler and ensure that it drinks plenty of water and, in some instances, its condition may warrant you dipping the chinchilla in a bowl of cool water up to its neck. This process should help to bring the animal's body temperature back to normal.

HAIR RING

This only occurs in male chinchillas, and is a ring of hair which develops around the penis, often due to repeated mating. The animal cannot remove the hair ring himself and so the penis is unable to be drawn back into the foreskin. If this condition is ignored, after some time the penis will waste away and it will cause the animal agonising pain and may result in a very painful death. For this reason, if your pet has mated and you notice afterwards it is very tired and perhaps cannot move or has lost interest in eating its food, you should check for signs of a hair ring. If so, you will need to remove it yourself by softening it with warm water, using perhaps a gentle lubricant of some kind, and then very carefully and very gently push the penis back into the foreskin.

Make sure you keep a check on the animal to ensure that no infection or irritation has developed, and that the chinchilla returns to its daily behaviour and activities without any further or recurring complications. Any signs of inflammation will indicate a problem, which must be treated by a vet to prevent any subsequent disorders.

ISOLATION

Whenever you are keeping two or more chinchillas together and one or more becomes sick, the sick

animal must be kept away from the others in a cage of its own. When cleaning the cage you should use completely different washing utensils.

If you buy a new chinchilla and wish to house it with other chinchillas you may have already, it is wise to keep them separated for a period of time, not only to allow them to get used to one another (once again by placing their cages side by side) but, more importantly, to reduce the risk of any infectious disease being spread.

CAGE CLEANLINESS

Maintaining the cage's cleanliness is essential in ensuring that your chinchilla stays fit and healthy throughout its life. Here are some very important factors to remember, which you may like to use as a checklist:

DAILY: Remove any food or hay which has fallen on to the bottom of the cage, as the chinchilla may eat these soiled and contaminated leftovers which could cause diarrhoea and other health problems.

Throw away any uneaten food and thoroughly wash the food container. Never re-use any leftover food which is in the bowl.

Empty any water left in the bottle and clean it thoroughly before filling it with fresh water. Never let the water become stale or stagnant as this will produce health problems for your chinchilla.

Remove all droppings from the dust bath and either stir or replace the chinchilla/silver sand, depending on how often the dust bath is used.

The litter tray will need cleaning on a weekly basis.

Wood shavings should be replaced.

Remove loose fur that has collected on the sides of the cage.

If using a wire-bottomed cage to house your chinchilla, you must replace the newspaper and/or wood shavings which line the metal or plastic tray.

WEEKLY: Empty the litter tray and replace with fresh wood shavings or bedding.

Remove any loose fur or clusters of fur which have collected on the sides and bottom of the cage.

Clean out the dust bath and replace with fresh chinchilla/silver sand.

TWICE A YEAR: It is a good idea to clean the cage thoroughly with a disinfectant, followed by rinsing with plenty of water or by using a blowlamp on wire cages.

Experienced owners may wish to breed from their chinchillas.

Careful consideration should be given to selecting a breeding pair.

Breeding Chinchillas

Since most people tend to keep chinchillas just as pets, either for themselves or their children, it is our intention to keep this section as simple but as informative as possible for those owners of chinchillas who want to increase the numbers and begin breeding them.

We will cover the most important areas of sex determination, the first meeting, mating, the pregnancy, the birth, after the birth, caring for the baby chinchilla, nursing and finally the weaning. Before starting to breed your chinchillas you must consider very carefully the implications of having more than one chinchilla and the risks involved.

SEX DETERMINATION

The first step in breeding is to determine the sex of your chinchilla, if you only have the one, and this is actually more complicated than you might think. It has been known for even experienced breeders to have made mistakes when determining the sex of their chinchillas.

Males and females have slightly different physiques – for example, the male chinchilla has a broader and larger head than the female, but its body is comparatively smaller. The sexual differences are not so straightforward. The female chinchilla has six nipples in total which are found on her abdomen (belly), in two straight lines of three, but they are not always easy to see unless the fur is parted. The female has a urethral cone, sometimes called the clitoris, which is often referred to as a 'false penis' due to its appearance and to its similarity to the male chinchilla's penis. The distance between the urethral cone and the anus is very small indeed, and the vagina is in the form of a horizontal slit. This is often very difficult to detect, as it remains closed unless the chinchilla is on heat, when it will open and be much easier to see. The male has a

A male chinchilla.

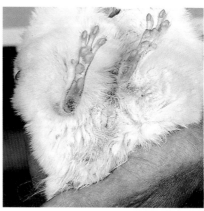

A female chinchilla.

larger gap between the penis and anus – usually about 1-1.5 cm.

Once you have determined the sex of your single chinchilla you will need to buy a suitable mate for it. Chinchillas recognise each other by their individual odour, which is not detectable by humans. Just as we get to know other people, it is important for chinchillas to get used to each other before attempting to mate them, and so it is suggested that you keep them in separate cages which are side by side for about a week. Once you feel they have had ample time to get accustomed to one another you may place them in the same cage.

THE FIRST MEETING

Next, it is important to watch how they react to one another, and this will usually start off with a period of curiosity and then perhaps a bit of playfulness. If this turns into more of an aggressive fight, you will need to separate them into the cages side by side once again, and allow them a little more time to get used to each other.

Sometimes the female may reject her intended mate and she will show her defensiveness by standing up on her hind legs and shooting urine at the intruder. If this aggressive behaviour is repeated after a week or so of being separated, then it will be necessary to replace the more volatile chinchilla. You may find that mating does not begin right away and this can be due to the chinchillas suffering from stress caused by being brought together in one cage.

MATING

At about 7-8 months of age, a female will become sexually active and has a 30-40 day cycle. The female chinchilla will not mate until she is ready to do so and until she feels comfortable with the situation and the area around her. By observing very closely, you will be able to determine when this is most likely to happen – usually when the male is more affectionate and responsive and the female is interested. The male chinchilla may even wag his tail and make a few noises.

When the female is finally ready, breeding will occur when she emits a wax-like vaginal plug. After copulation, the male will emit a wax-like substance into the vagina of the female, where it solidifies and keeps the semen inside for some time. Often, you may find a 'copulatory plug' on the bottom of the cage – this is the excess sperm which has been emitted from the vagina and is an indication that mating has occurred.

Once intercourse has taken place, it is very important for you to check that the male has not

The chinchillas may take some time to accept each other.

developed a hair ring. If you find this is the case, then you will need to follow the necessary procedures as outlined in Chapter Six.

PREGNANCY

The full gestation period or length of pregnancy is 111 days, and it is usually exact to within a couple of days. There are a few dos and don'ts during this period, which are of the utmost importance if the birth is to be successful.

DO leave the male and female together during the full term of the pregnancy because the male will act as a caring father after the birth and will dry the babies and keep them warm. It is probably best to remove him from the cage for the first few days following the birth, however, as the female will come on heat again.

DO increase the food supply during the pregnancy in order to provide nutrients and to maintain the pregnant chinchilla's strength if she appears to want extra food, but do not worry if she does not as it is quite common for females to lose their appetite and refuse their food for a while, and they may even lose some weight. You should not be too concerned by this because this is very natural for many pregnant female chinchillas.

DO increase the amount of water available just a few days before giving birth.

DON'T ever take the female away from her natural environment or place her in another cage because this what she has grown accustomed to. This is very dangerous and can have disastrous consequences – it has been known for females who have been moved from one cage to another to abort and then eat the dead babies.

DON'T ever hold the female chinchilla while she is pregnant – this could stress her and affect the development of the foetus/es. For this reason you must leave her in peace. If it becomes absolutely necessary to hold her you must ensure that you support the rear end and never lift her by the tail, which could result in her aborting.

DON'T attempt to assist the female during the birth – this is a natural process for her. Even if there are signs of a few complications there is no need to panic.

DON'T allow your female chinchilla to have a dust bath on the due date of the birth – by knowing the gestation period it is possible to work out an almost exact date. Any bacteria present in the sand could cause an inflammation of the womb or vagina.

THE BIRTH

Most births usually occur in the morning with the labour period lasting only a short while followed by the birth, which, if it is multiple, could last for a few hours. Ensure that the room in which the cage is placed is warm enough, unless you are providing some sort of heated nest box. This is only used if the room is not centrally heated and consists of a wooden box which is attached to the side of the cage, which must be large enough for the mother and her newborns to fit inside. The box has two sections, the top one being where the chinchillas will go to keep warm and the second, which is underneath and contains a 15-watt bulb. You must, of course, ensure that the

A nesting box should be provided for the pregnant doe.

flex from the bulb is completely outside the cage to prevent the chinchillas from nibbling on it. Generally nest boxes are only used in extremely cold climates.

With the onset of labour, the mother will stretch, perspire and make painful labouring sounds, followed by the emission of fluid from the sac around the baby chinchilla. As her young are born, the mother will help by carefully pulling them out with her teeth and then she will wash and dry each new one with the aid of her thick fur. Most female chinchillas give birth to two babies, but it is not uncommon for them to have three.

After the birth, the male should be removed from the cage to prevent a further mating taking place.

AFTER THE BIRTH

For every baby there is always one placenta and it may be hard to believe but it is perfectly natural and common for the mother to eat the afterbirth. We touched very briefly on the fact that many who eat the afterbirth suffer from digestive problems. Evidence of the afterbirth not only being delivered but also eaten is provided simply if you can see any blood on the mother's nose and paws. Generally, the cage will appear very clean.

We said earlier that there is no harm in keeping the male and female together even after the birth – however, it is probably best to remove him for the first three days or so. The reason for this is because the female actually goes into heat only 24 hours after giving birth and so the male will try to mate again. If he is successful there is a possibility that the female will become pregnant again too soon, and she will find it too exhausting to be pregnant with one litter and to be also nursing the other. For this reason, it is not advisable to allow them to mate so soon after the birth. It is safe to return the male to the female and newborns after a few days so that he can resume his fatherly role.

CARING FOR BABIES

It is not normal for a mother to abandon or reject her babies and hence fail to carry out her motherly duties. However, first-time breeders will know that this has happened if the mother ignores her young immediately after birth, failing to wash and dry them with her fur. You will notice the newborn chinchillas lying unclean, cold and motionless on the bottom of the cage. Breeders are not certain why some mothers reject their babies, but it could be because the birthing procedure is not finished. If abandonment does occur, you must assist in caring for her newborn or they will not survive.

To do this, you must take the baby (or 'kit' as it is sometimes known) and place it gently in some warm water up to its neck, and then carefully rub its body for a little while. Wrap it in a towel to keep it warm until you put it back in the cage with its mother. This procedure should revive the newborn, but there have been some cases of breeders having to

use artificial respiration – this is done by taking the baby in one hand and, with the other, making a small fist close to your mouth and then making very short breaths close to the mouth of the infant. Do not breathe directly into the mouth of the newborn as this would be far too strong.

Not only are chinchillas born with their eyes already open and their body covered with fur, but they also have a full set of teeth. These are white in colour initially, but later will develop the distinctive yellow colour. You will probably have to get their teeth filed down before they begin to nurse, which prevents them from injuring their mother or themselves as they playfully choose a nipple from which they get their milk. Although the mother should not mind you holding the babies, it is important that you have a vet show you the correct way to file their teeth before you attempt to do so yourself. Baby chinchillas are born without claws but these will develop as it grows.

NURSING

Chinchillas are quite different to dogs, cats and rabbits when they nurse their young because the mother chinchilla does not lie down, but instead allows access to her nipples by standing up on her hind legs. Most mothers have enough milk for up to three babies, so you will probably not need to supplement it in any way. If, however, the litter is large, then it is suggested that you allow the babies to nurse for two hours at a time before they stay with the mother permanently. It is common for newborns to begin nursing about 12 hours after birth, because they already have a supply of food when they are born. A happy and healthy baby chinchilla will often curl its tail while nursing.

WEANING

Weaning normally begins at around 6-8 weeks and is completed after 10-11 weeks, when it will be normal for the young chinchillas to drink water on the same scale as the adults, but it is important to ensure that they do not overeat. Only allow them half the rations of an adult. It is a common mistake for some breeders to give the young chinchillas too much food, which can lead to certain health problems such as diarrhoea and

Baby chinchillas are not fully weaned until 10-11 weeks of age.

maybe even death. Always maintain a check on their health and once they reach the age of five or six months, then you can allow them to have the normal amount of adult food. Sometimes it is quite possible for the mother to produce milk, even after her young have been weaned, and, if this is so, it will be necessary to return them to the mother for a couple more feeds.

It is highly recommended that you leave the mother for a period of four weeks or so before you attempt the breeding process once again. To assess and establish her level of fitness and state of health, it is extremely important that you watch her closely, and ascertain whether or not she is behaving in a normal fashion and displaying good and regular eating habits. It is vital that the female chinchilla returns to normal after the birth, which will prove that she has not been adversely affected by the pregnancy. You should only make the decision to try and mate her again when you feel comfortable

During the weaning period, it is important that the young chinchillas do not over-eat.

about her state of health and general behaviour. Please bear in mind that, although you may feel it is time for her to breed again, she may not, so a little extra time may be needed.

Now it is time to learn how to become a good friend and companion to your chinchilla!

Names
and Games

For many people who decide to have a pet, the most common problem is that once you have got your pet back home you cannot decide on a name for it. It can be quite a dilemma, particularly if your family cannot agree, so your pet may remain without a name for some time. It is not very fair to have a nameless animal; after all, how will it be able to respond to you when you try to call it? It cannot respond to its name if it has not got one!

Some people choose a name which reflects their pet's size, such as Bruno or Tyson, or perhaps their colouring, such as Brownie or Blackie. For most, it is a difficult decision and sometimes a name, out of the blue, just sticks. We thought we would make this part of the book fun, and for this we had to dig deep into our imaginations to come up with a few suggestions. You may decide to choose a name from our list or you may have already thought up a few of your own. Either way we wish you the best of luck in choosing a name for your chinchilla.

FEMALE NAMES

Peach, Lily, Daisy, Tinkerbell, Ruby, Cameo, Honey, Harriett, Lucy, Pixie, Fluffy, Chloe, Jemima, Candy, Princess, Moonlight, Rosie, Beauty, Matilda, Crystal, Pattie, Chica, Flamenco, Cinderella, Tabitha, Sissy, Angelica, Petra, Georgia, Martha, Nellie, Marmalade, Lavender, Bessie, Pearl, Duchess, Polly, Bonnie, Royale, Sugar and Esther.

MALE NAMES

Cheeky, Spider, Ben, Chester, Moses, Reggie, Guinness, Morris, Ringo, Prince, Mercury, Roland, Denver, Elliot, Pepper, Hamlet, Barney, Toby, Roger, Sebastian, Custard, Buster, Maxi, Napoleon, Zebedee, Oscar, Gus, Ferdinand, Isaac, George, Harry, Ronnie, Gareth, Bobbie, Ziggy, Rufus, Quincey, Herbert, Chico, Lionel and Sidney.

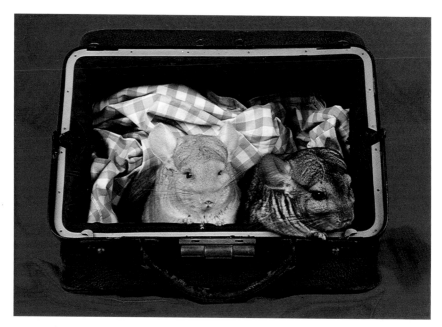

HAVING FUN

As with any pet, whether it be a dog, a cat or a chinchilla, the most important thing is to gain their trust. If they feel comfortable with the way you handle them and treat them then they will be happy. Pets are not toys that can be forgotten when you become bored or fed up – they can be very demanding and hard work but, above all, a lot of fun. You do not necessarily have to take your chinchilla out of the cage for you or it to have fun. They will provide hours of entertainment by playing with their toys or just by rolling around in their dust bath.

INTRODUCTIONS

Just as we introduce ourselves to people we meet for the first time, it is important that you do the same with chinchillas. They are naturally very timid animals and will only nibble at your fingers (as opposed to giving you a nasty bite) unless provoked.

Regardless of the age of the chinchilla, you must let it get used to you, and this can be achieved by initially allowing it to sniff your hand so that each time you approach it or hold it, it will recognise that same smell and identify it as being you. You must remember that newborn chinchillas will be very scared if you try to hold them, so it is better to wait until they are older and more confident and curious before attempting to take them out of the cage. You should slowly place your hand inside the cage, taking care not to make any sudden or jerky movements, which will scare the chinchilla, or to make any loud noises. Being a curious creature, the chinchilla will come over to inspect your hand, have a sniff and then go away again. After a while it will become accustomed to you and eventually play around your hand. You may decide to end each little visit with a treat of some kind,

but ensure that treats are given at regular times.

Once the chinchilla is happy with you, it will allow you to lift it out of the cage and this is where the fun time can begin.

TRICKS

Chinchillas are very much like squirrels and rabbits in that they are extremely clever and can often be taught to do certain tricks such as sitting up and begging, jumping and even responding when you call them by their name. Just as most owners like to reward their pets for something well done, so you too can reward your chinchilla with a treat or even perhaps an affectionate scratch under the chin or behind the ears.

It is important to separate fun

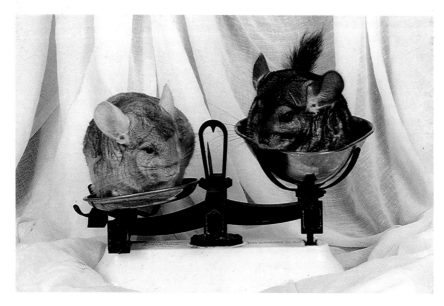

time from training time as this can cause undue stress to the animal, and, if you find that at any time the chinchilla appears tired and just wants to lie down, then this is a good time to stop the activity you are doing. When training your chinchilla it is better to do it inside, as outside you might find there are too many distractions and the session becomes a waste of time.

INDIVIDUALITY

Like most animals, and indeed ourselves, in time you will notice that chinchillas will develop their own characteristics and personality. This is very important to remember, especially if you have more than one, because, whereas one will enjoy being held and scratched, another will enjoy playing and being adventurous. You must make allowances for a chinchilla's individuality and you should not expect it to behave in the same way as the next chinchilla.

Also available in the Pet Owner's Guide series

*A comprehensive guide to caring for a pet rabbit.
Price £4.99*

*Choosing a hamster, diet, housing and breeding hamsters are examined in detail.
Price £4.99*

For a complete list of Britain's best pet books, write to:
**Ringpress Books, P.O. Box 8, Lydney, Gloucestershire, GL15 4YN.
Tel 01594 845577   Fax 01594 845599**

*A complete guide to help the novice look after this fascinating pet.
Price £4.99*